Editor	Karen Barker Smith
Editorial Assistant	Stephanie Cole
Artists	David Ansty
	Giovanni Caselli
	Nick Hewetson
	Carolyn Scrace
	David Stewart
	Kareen Taylerson

Author

Jacqueline Morley studied English at Oxford University. She has taught English and History and has a special interest in the history of everyday life. She has written historical fiction and non-fiction for children and is the author of the prize-winning **An Egyptian Pyramid** in the *Inside Story* series.

Series creator

David Salariya was born in Dundee, Scotland, where he studied illustration and printmaking. He has illustrated a wide range of books on botanical, historical and mythological subjects. He has created over 150 books for publishers in the UK and overseas. In 1989 he set up The Salariya Book Company. He lives in Brighton with his wife, the illustrator Shirley Willis, and their son Jonathan.

Created, designed and produced by
THE SALARIYA BOOK COMPANY LTD
25 Marlborough Place, Brighton BN1 1UB

ISBN 0 7500 2738 X

Published in 1999 by Macdonald Young Books,
an imprint of Wayland Publishers Ltd
61 Western Road, Hove BN3 1JD

You can find Macdonald Young Books on the internet at:
http://www.myb.co.uk

A CIP catalogue record for this book is available from
the British Library.

Printed in Hong Kong.

Look & Wonder

Signs of the Zodiac

Created and designed by
David Salariya

Written by
Jacqueline Morley

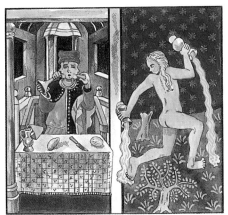

MACDONALD YOUNG BOOKS

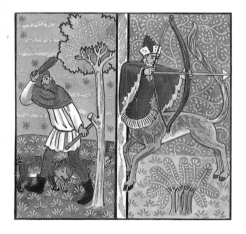

Contents

Map of the zodiac

The twelve signs of the zodiac are ancient symbols. They are still known today through their use in astrology – the study of the apparent influence of the sun and planets on people's lives. Magazine horoscopes have made us familiar with the idea that everyone is born under the influence of one of these signs and this suggests that the origins of the zodiac were magical and mysterious. However, even though the zodiac has been shrouded in magic and mystery for over two thousand years, it was invented for an entirely practical purpose – to accurately measure time.

The word 'zodiac' is Greek, meaning 'a circle of animals' – all the signs but one are living creatures. The zodiac is an imaginary band of sky encircling the Earth. It is the path along which the sun appears to travel in the course of a year. The sun does not really circle the Earth, it is the Earth that circles the sun, but stargazers in ancient times were unaware of that. They saw that the sun crossed the sky against a background of stars which did not move. Before clocks were invented the only way to know the time of day was to see how near the sun was to setting. Similarly, the only way to tell how much of the year had passed was to see how far the sun had travelled on its yearly journey.

At first, stars were used as markers. For instance, when a certain star was visible with the sun at dawn or dusk farmers would know it was time to prepare the land for crops. But astronomers needed a more accurate way to measure time, so they divided the sun's circuit into twelve equal sections and it is these that form the zodiac.

Certain stars seem to form groups ('constellations') in the sky. Long before the zodiac was thought of, these were given names – the Lion, the Ram, etc. Some names were suggested by the shape of the star groups and some were named to honour gods. In naming each zodiac section, astronomers borrowed the name of a constellation in that part of the sky.

This diagram (right) shows the globe as if one were looking in from outside the universe, through transparent walls.

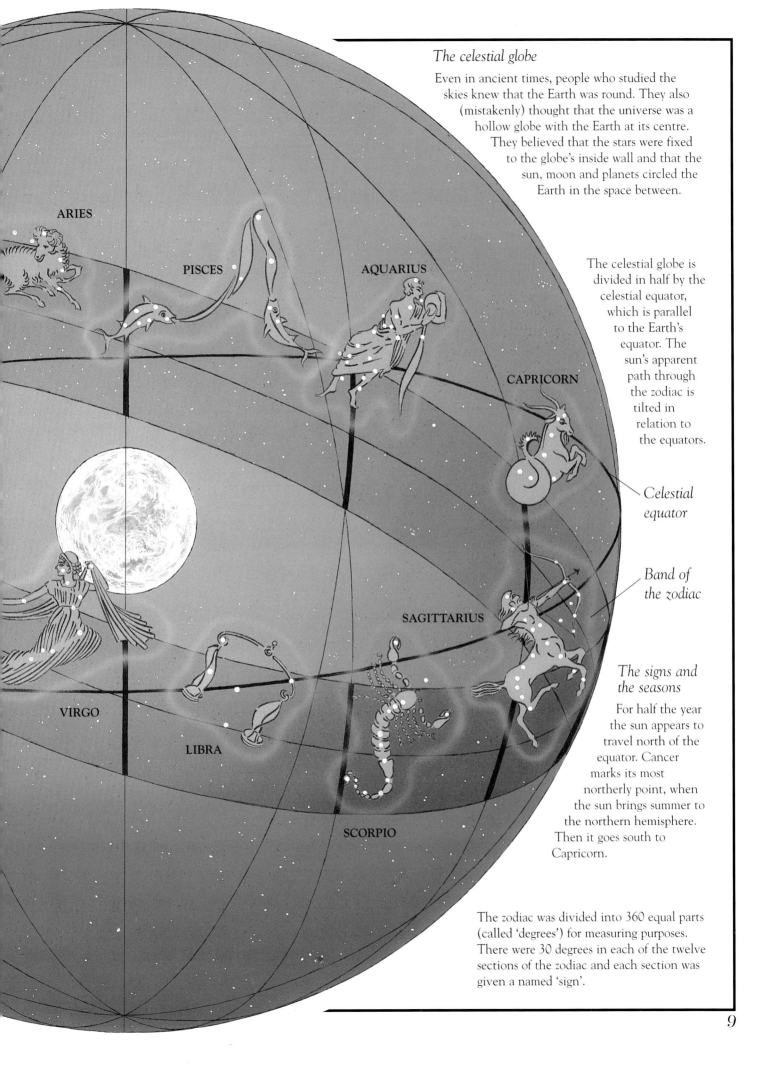

ARIES

PISCES

AQUARIUS

CAPRICORN

VIRGO

LIBRA

SCORPIO

SAGITTARIUS

The celestial globe

Even in ancient times, people who studied the skies knew that the Earth was round. They also (mistakenly) thought that the universe was a hollow globe with the Earth at its centre. They believed that the stars were fixed to the globe's inside wall and that the sun, moon and planets circled the Earth in the space between.

The celestial globe is divided in half by the celestial equator, which is parallel to the Earth's equator. The sun's apparent path through the zodiac is tilted in relation to the equators.

Celestial equator

Band of the zodiac

The signs and the seasons

For half the year the sun appears to travel north of the equator. Cancer marks its most northerly point, when the sun brings summer to the northern hemisphere. Then it goes south to Capricorn.

The zodiac was divided into 360 equal parts (called 'degrees') for measuring purposes. There were 30 degrees in each of the twelve sections of the zodiac and each section was given a named 'sign'.

Looking at the sky

A Babylonian god pours streams of water (above). The idea of Aquarius, the pourer of the waters of life, is a very ancient one.

A Babylonian astronomical instrument of the 7th century BC (below). It was used to measure the positions of the stars.

Symbols of the sun, the moon and Venus appear at the top of a Babylonian relief of c. 1300 BC (below). It is probable that the scorpion also represented a sky god.

Long ago, people watched the sky and believed the lights in it were gods. They noted how the sky rotated daily from east to west, yet in it some stars were fixed while others were moving, wandering slowly eastwards against the background pattern of the rest. The movements of the seven wandering stars (sun, moon and five visible planets) were seen as signals from the gods.

The stargazers of ancient Babylon were skilled astronomers: by observing the sun and moon they worked out an accurate calendar of days, months and years. They also kept records, over hundreds of years, of the positions of the stars at various times, and of accompanying events which happened, they believed, as a result. This enabled them to tell their rulers what the movements in the sky foretold. It was assumed that the stars only held messages of importance concerning kingdoms, wars and natural disasters. The idea that each person has an individual star-destiny did not arise until the invention of the zodiac, around 400 BC.

Babylonian versions of Sagittarius, Capricorn and Aquarius (above). Sagittarius has the tail of a scorpion; Capricorn has a fish's tail and Aquarius is female.

This Syrian clay tablet (left) of 200 BC records the earliest known horoscope: 'the place of Venus means wherever he may go it will be favourable; he will have sons and daughters.'

A scorpion-tailed archer appears on a Babylonian boundary marker (above) of the 12th century BC. At this early date the figure may not refer to the constellation Sagittarius, but it is clearly the supernatural being after whom the constellation was named.

An eclipse of the sun (when the moon passes in front of it) was believed to be a warning of some great event or disaster affecting kings and empires. Rulers expected their astrologers to warn them when eclipses of the sun or moon were going to happen.

Ancient Egyptian zodiac

The zodiac was worked out over the centuries by Babylonian astronomer-astrologers. (There was no distinction then between astronomy, which studies the physical nature of the stars and planets and astrology, which interprets the apparent meaning of their movements). They noticed that the seven wandering 'stars' all made their yearly circuit within the same band of sky and passed across the same fixed constellations. They did not know that all but the sun were planets.

The Babylonians were convinced that the influence of each of the seven altered according to the stages of their journey. The stages were marked by the constellations, but these occupied unequal areas of sky so were not an efficient means of measuring.

The names of the constellations were linked to the gods, though their exact meaning is hard to interpret. The Egyptians used Babylonian names for most of the zodiac constellations but kept their own for Aries the Ram, which honoured their god Amun (right).

The zodiac, an imaginary division of the sky into equal parts, enabled astronomers to pinpoint exactly where the seven stars would be at any given moment and to measure their relationships to each other. This accuracy then allowed them to give a minute by minute account of the influence of the stars on human affairs. From there it was a short step to studying the effects on individual people, depending on the state of the sky at the moment of their birth. This was known as a horoscope.

The earliest Babylonian text to mention the zodiac dates from c. 410 BC. It seems that the Greeks learned about the zodiac from the Babylonians and introduced it to Egypt. The Greek-built city of Alexandria in Egypt became a famous centre of learning, where astrologers worked out elaborate systems of interpretation for the zodiac, using ideas from Babylon, Egypt and Greece.

An Egyptian zodiac ceiling painted in AD 17 (above). The figures on it represent the constellations the Egyptians identified in the sky. The twelve zodiac constellations are there along with several others. The figures marching around the rim of the circle are 'decans' (see right).

Part of an Egyptian zodiac frieze (below), c. 221 BC shows Libra, Scorpio and Sagittarius. The dog-headed figures represent 'decans'. The Egyptians divided the year into thirty-six ten-day 'weeks' called decans. The Egyptians put the decans into the zodiac, three to a sign. They believed each decan influenced the star that was passing through it.

The figures on an Egyptian 'sky map' from about 1250 BC (above) represent constellations that were important to the ancient Egyptians. The bull here represents the constellation now known as the Plough.

Aries

21 March to 20 April

Aries, the Ram, is a fire sign, ruled by Mars. Aries is the first of the twelve signs because it marks the beginning of spring in the northern hemisphere, where the zodiac of the western world was invented. 21 March is the date when the sun crosses the equator going north.

The ancient Greeks associated each zodiac sign with a character from their myths as they believed this is where the zodiac names originated. The ram of the ancient Greek zodiac is the golden ram which appeared from the skies to rescue Phrixus and Helle. Their unhappy father was about to sacrifice them to the gods to end a terrible famine which he thought the gods had sent. He did not know his children's wicked stepmother had caused it, by roasting all the seedcorn so that the crops could not sprout. Zeus, king of the gods, saw it all and sent the ram just in time. It took Phrixus and Helle on its back and flew with them to the faraway land of Colchis. There Phrixus sacrificed the ram to Zeus to thank him and presented its glittering fleece to the king of Colchis. The king hung it in a sacred grove, where it was guarded day and night by a dragon that never slept.

Basic Personality

Arians are adventurous, energetic, brave, enthusiastic and always lively. They are great fun to be around. However, selfishness and impatience are typical Arian faults, as well as their hot temper when provoked!

Ideal Job

Arians do not like office work and are better suited to more exciting jobs, such as fireman, racing driver, sportsperson or actor.

Favourite Hobbies

All types of sport and outdoor activities keep Arians entertained. They are also good at singing and dancing.

Lifestyle

Arians at home like to be the centre of attention and always want to be in charge. They tend to boss brothers and sisters around and are often in trouble for being noisy. However, they are also very entertaining and good at telling jokes as a way to get back in favour.

Colours	Creature	Flower	Gemstone	Food	Place	People
Bright colours are always Arian favourites, but best of all are red and bright pink.	The ram and sheep are commonly associated with Aries.	Traditional Arian plants include the thistle, bryony and honeysuckle.	The Arian gemstone is the magnificent diamond – the bigger the better!	Arians' favourite meals are usually hot and spicy. They like curries and chillies and are also fond of onions and leeks.	Arian countries include England, France and Germany. Favourite towns are Verona and Florence in Italy.	Arians get along well with Leo and Sagittarius people but not so well with Capricorns or Librans.

Taurus

21 April to 21 May

Basic Personality

Taureans are very sensible people, full of practical common sense. They are very good at listening and giving advice and make extremely loyal and caring friends. Greed and occasional moodiness are a Taurean's worst faults.

Ideal Job

Taureans are ambitious and eager to earn lots of money. They often achieve great success in business and finance, but they are also often musically talented – many famous singers are Taureans.

Favourite Hobbies

Entertaining friends at extravagant dinners and parties is a popular Taurean pastime, as well as gardening and drawing.

Lifestyle

Collecting ornaments is a common Taurean habit and their bedrooms often look very untidy and cluttered, although they are usually very well organised.

Taurus, the Bull, is an earth sign ruled by Venus. The constellation that gave the sign its name does not seem to have been recognised as a bull by the Babylonians, but the Greeks named that group of stars as early as the 5th century BC.

The ancient Greeks said the bull in their zodiac was in fact Zeus, king of the gods, who transformed himself into a bull in order to carry off his love, the princess Europa. One day, as Europa was strolling with friends along the seashore she saw that her father's cattle had broken out of their pasture and were wandering on the sand. Among them was a magnificent bull with horns that shone like the crescent moon. When the bull came up and nuzzled her hand, she stroked its silky flanks and made a garland for its neck. As it knelt down meekly she clambered on its back and called to her friends to join her. But the bull did not want any other passengers. It plunged into the waves and carried Europa out to sea. Europa's brother Cadmus searched the world to find her. He went at last to the famous oracle at Delphi to hear the god Apollo. "Abandon your search," the oracle told him. "Your sister is the bride of Zeus and will never be restored to you." Cadmus knew his quest was hopeless, for no one can reclaim what the gods have stolen.

Colours	Creature	Flower	Gemstone	Food	Place	People
Typical Taurean colours are pink, pale blue and pale green.	The bull is the original Taurean creature but all cattle are traditionally associated with this sign.	Taurean flowers include the foxglove, rose, poppy, daisy and violet.	The green emerald is the Taurean gemstone.	Taureans love exotic or luxurious food and also have a very sweet tooth. Chocolate is usually a big favourite!	Ireland, Greece and Switzerland are Taurean countries and Dublin is a favourite city.	Taureans get on best with Capricorns and Virgos but can have problems with both Leos and Scorpios.

The classical zodiac

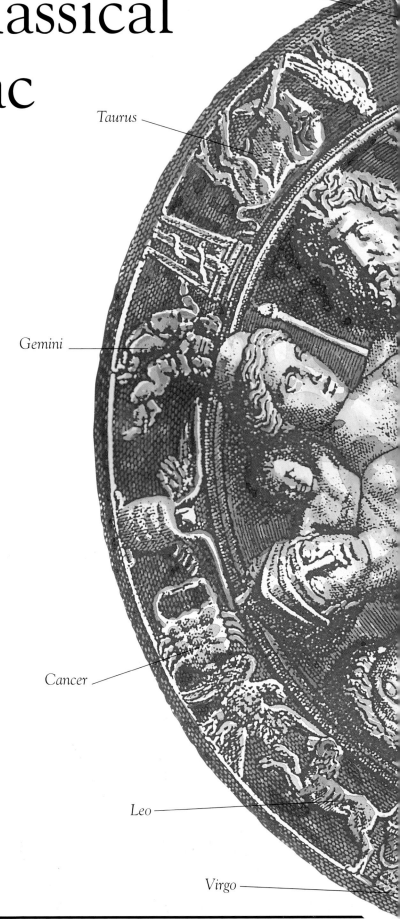

Aries

Taurus

Gemini

Cancer

Leo

Virgo

Greek astrologers increased the range of meaning in the zodiac enormously by defining all sorts of relationships between the signs and the seven stars that moved through them. There were countless variations, each with its effect on human character and fate – complicated mathematics were often needed to work them out.

Travelling astrologers brought the zodiac to Rome around 200 BC. Educated Romans regarded it with suspicion at first as a new Greek idea. The statesman Cicero called it 'improbable nonsense which is daily disproved by experience'. He argued that a newborn baby was more likely to be influenced by the weather than by the zodiac – at least it could feel the weather! But eventually, the idea of a personal fate, decipherable in the sky, proved too attractive for most Romans to resist.

Many Greek astrologers wrote learned works on the subject. The most influential was by Ptolemy, in the 2nd century AD. His textbook 'Tetrabiblos' put a great deal of confused astrological theory into order and was used for centuries.

The Romans assigned their gods and goddesses to the signs of the zodiac: Minerva, goddess of wisdom to Aries; Venus goddess of love to Taurus; Apollo, god of poetry and music to Gemini; Mercury the messenger to Cancer; Jupiter, king of the gods, to Leo; Ceres the corn goddess to Virgo; Vulcan the blacksmith to Libra; Diana the moon goddess to Sagittarius; Mars, god of war, to Scorpio; Vesta, goddess of the hearth, to Capricorn; Saturn, god of time to Aquarius and the sea god Neptune to Pisces.

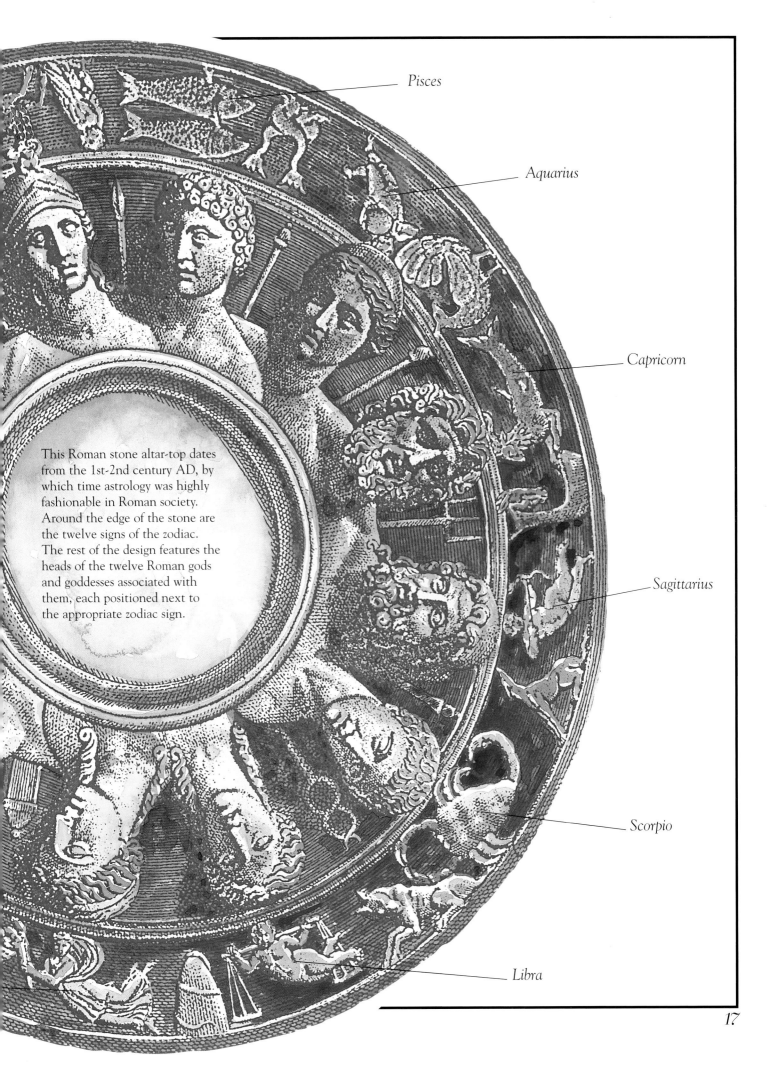

Pisces

Aquarius

Capricorn

This Roman stone altar-top dates from the 1st-2nd century AD, by which time astrology was highly fashionable in Roman society. Around the edge of the stone are the twelve signs of the zodiac. The rest of the design features the heads of the twelve Roman gods and goddesses associated with them, each positioned next to the appropriate zodiac sign.

Sagittarius

Scorpio

Libra

Zodiac motifs were popular as decoration. This Roman roof finial (below right) is flanked by two Capricorn-like creatures.

Silver coinage (below) issued by the emperor Augustus bore the sign of Capricorn, under which he had been born.

Zodiac signs surround a figure from a shrine to the god Mithras (below), the Lord of Time. Many Romans worshipped this Middle Eastern god.

Roman astrology

By imperial times most Romans were addicted to astrology. The emperors had court astrologers and these could have a major influence on policy. Useful information might be gained by reading someone else's horoscope. In AD 11, Emperor Augustus made it illegal to try to discover when someone else would die. Some would-be fashionable Romans became obsessed with astrology. They could not even take a bath (it was said) without consulting their personal astrologer. The writer Petronius makes fun of this craze in his comic novel, 'The Satyricon', in which he describes a preposterous banquet given by Trimalchio, a man with more money than sense. Each dish of the main course represented a zodiac sign.

On Trimalchio's zodiac platter Taurus was a piece of beef, Gemini a pair of kidneys, Scorpio a crawfish and so on (below).

In the middle of the platter, a lump of turf symbolised the Earth.

Gemini

22 May to 21 June

Gemini is an air sign, ruled by Mercury. The constellation of Gemini, the Twins, contains two stars which are particularly bright. One shines even brighter than the other, which reflects the associated story of the ancient Greek heroes, Castor and Pollux.

Castor and Pollux were devoted twins. Though Pollux was immortal and Castor was not, there was no jealousy between them. One time they went cattle-raiding with their cousins Lyncheus and Idas and fell out over sharing the spoils. The twins felt cheated so they seized all the cattle and waited inside a hollow oak to ambush their cousins. But Lyncheus had the power to see through the tree and warned his brother, who hurled a spear into the trunk and through Castor's body. Pollux took his dying brother in his arms, lamenting that he must live forever without him. Zeus offered him a choice: to join the gods on Mount Olympus or to share death with his brother. Pollux immediately chose death, so Zeus allowed the twins to spend half their time in the underworld among the dead and half in happiness with the gods.

Basic Personality

Geminis are versatile people who are always curious about the world around them. They are great talkers and like nothing more than the chance to tell people their ideas and opinions. Unpredictability is a common Gemini fault. They also get bored easily and tend to leave tasks half finished.

Ideal Job

Anything that involves talking and communicating, such as teaching, writing, selling or advertising.

Favourite Hobbies

Geminis love reading and often spend lots of time writing letters to friends and speaking on the telephone.

Lifestyle

A Gemini will be the talker of the family and likes to be surrounded by other people. He or she is one of the rare people who like to share a room with a brother or sister.

Flower	Creature	Colour	Gemstone	Food	Places	People
Lily-of-the-Valley, lavender and myrtle are Gemini flowers.	Any talking birds, such as parrots, are associated with Gemini, as is the quick-witted monkey.	Geminis love bright colours, particularly yellow.	Agate is the Gemini gemstone.	Geminis are not too fussy about food. The most important thing is variety. A Gemini is always keen to try new things.	Wales is a Gemini favourite, as is its capital, Cardiff.	Librans and Aquarians are good friends for Geminis.

Cancer

22 June to 22 July

Cancer is a water sign. When the sun is at its most northerly point in the sky it seems to hover and then change direction to take a southward path. This movement, rather like the sideways shuffle of a crab, may have suggested the symbol. The ancient Greeks were probably the first to call it the Crab.

The zodiac crab refers to the one that tackled the hero Heracles. It was sent by his enemy Hera, queen of the gods, who had always hated him. Knowing her husband, Zeus, had been in love with Heracles' mother and, suspecting Heracles to be his son, she vowed to destroy him. She cursed him with a fit of madness in which he slew his wife and children, mistaking them for enemies. As penance for this the gods ordered him to become the servant of his cousin Eurystheus and perform whatever tasks he set. Among other dangerous tasks, he sent Heracles to kill the Hydra, a monstrous watersnake which ate people and cattle. The nine-headed Hydra coiled itself around Heracles so that he could barely move. Then Hera's monster, an enormous crab, came scuttling out and fastened its pincers on Heracles' foot. With a furious stamp he crushed its shell to pieces. Hera rewarded her loyal crab with a place among the stars.

Basic Personality

Cancerians are very kind and caring people, who are often also imaginative and creative. However, bad moods and hot tempers are common in Cancerians. If someone upsets them they will sulk for days!

Ideal Job

Cancerians are blessed with shrewd business skills but often choose caring professions, such as nursing or teaching young children.

Favourite Hobbies

Cancerians are natural hoarders and often like to collect things. They also enjoy swimming and dancing.

Lifestyle

Messiness is a typical Cancerian trait and the state of their room can be a cause for family arguments!

Flower	Creature	Colour	Gemstone	Food	Place	People
Any white flower is traditionally Cancerian, in particular geraniums, lilies and white roses.	Animals which have shells are usually Cancerian, but the crab is the most obvious one.	Cancer is linked to smoky grey and silver colours.	The Cancerian gemstone is the pearl.	Cancerians have big appetites and enjoy most food, although they particularly like dairy produce.	Holland is a Cancerian country and its capital, Amsterdam, is also ruled by this sign.	Cancerians get on best with Scorpios, Pisceans and Leos.

Medieval zodiac

A 16th-century magician's magic circle (above) was made of zodiac symbols.

*T*he early Christian Church denounced astrology as a pagan superstition. Also, the idea of a fate arranged by the stars conflicted with the fundamental Christian concept that all of us are free to act as we choose and therefore we alone are responsible for our actions, good or bad. Yet gradually astrological ideas were blended with the Christian faith. The signs could be given a Christian meaning: the Ram as the Lamb of God; The Twins as the Old and New Testaments; Virgo, the Virgin Mary; Aquarius, the waters of Baptism. Medieval church porches often show the zodiac signs as symbols of time and they were commonly used to illustrate the popular medieval theme of a year's work in the countryside.

A 15th-century French version of the zodiac year (opposite):
Aries – pruning new shoots on the vines.
Taurus – the man carries a branch from which he will cut shoots for grafting.
Gemini – a falconer rides with his bird on his wrist.
Cancer – mowing for hay.
Leo – cutting ripe corn.
Virgo – threshing corn.
Libra – trampling grapes for wine-making.
Scorpio – the ploughed land is sown for a crop next year.
Sagittarius – pigs are driven out to fatten on acorns.
Capricorn – killing a pig for a feast.
Aquarius – the approach of the year's end is shown by a two-faced figure. One of his faces looks to the future.
Pisces – resting before a fire.

Aquarius (above) and Pisces (below) of 1497, from a set of twelve signs sculpted on an arch at Merton College, Oxford.

Sagittarius from the zodiac sculptures in Merton College arch (left). In a Christian setting the signs came to symbolise the endless cycle of time.

A late 15th-century manuscript painting sets the birth of Christ at the centre of the zodiac (right). The idea of Christ as the Light of the World and the Lord of Time made zodiac symbolism acceptable in medieval times. Some Christians reasoned that perhaps the stars really did provide signs – a star guided the wise men to Bethlehem.

Pisces (above) could be interpreted as a Christian sign, as a fish was an early Christian symbol for Christ.

Aries

Taurus

Gemini

Cancer

Leo

Virgo

Libra

Scorpio

Sagittarius

Capricorn

Aquarius

Pisces

23

The planets

Only the seven moving lights visible to the naked eye (the planets) had meaning in early astrology. Interpreting the combined influences of all seven was a complex task. The theory was that the planets interact and alter each other's influence, but the nature of their interaction is never the same. It varies according to the position in the zodiac of each planet in relation to the rest. As all travel at different speeds their relationships constantly change. Particular distances between planets make them enemies or friends and alter their effects. When more planets were found (Uranus in 1781, Neptune in 1846 and Pluto in 1930) relationships were reallocated and new effects detected. Rather than leading to queries of their beliefs, astrologers saw this as explanation of incorrect predictions in the past.

These are 15th-century Italian portraits of the 'Seven Stars', showing the activities they influence. Mars (below), the ruler of Aries and Scorpio, is a fierce, unfriendly 'star', though its harm is lessened if it is in a friendly relationship with one or more of the others. It brings energy, adventure, courage, enthusiasm, success, war, ruthlessness and brutality.

Mercury (left), the ruler of Gemini and Virgo, is the nimblest of the 'stars' and darts around the zodiac. It is the star of communication: talking, writing and creating new ideas. Mercury is also associated with liveliness of mind, trade, business skills, curiosity, competitiveness and cunning.

Saturn (right), the ruler of Aquarius and Capricorn, is the slowest star – it takes 29.5 years to make its way round the zodiac. It is cold by nature and suggests remoteness and mystery. Its influence is associated with stern control, caution, perseverance, depression, learning and old age.

·SATVRNVS·

·VENVS·

The Moon (above), which rules Cancer, affects people's emotional response to life, their feelings for those who are dear to them, their daily habits and innermost needs. It is the star of motherhood, dreams, bodily health, thoughtfulness, cooperation, memories, water and the seas.

Venus (left), the ruler of Taurus and Libra, is usually a friendly star. It influences love, feminine beauty, home life, pleasure, children, art, wealth, energy, imagination, harmony and renewal.

·SOL·

The Sun (left) that rules the fire sign of Leo represents life force, authority, vitality and self expression. Its position indicates how a person's energies will be best used. It brings justice, power, will, determination, pride, luck, creativity and love of display.

Jupiter, the ruler (until reallocation) of Pisces and Sagittarius, is a smiling, fruitful star, causing feelings of emotional expansion and optimism. It brings wealth, ownership, travel, a strong moral sense, humour, generosity, an honourable reputation, victory and fame.

·IVPITER·

Leo

24 July to 23 August

Leo is a fire sign ruled by the Sun. It seems that the pattern of stars in this sign has always reminded people of a large animal with its tail outstretched. In China it was seen as a horse, in South America, as a puma leaping on its prey. In some Babylonian texts it is called a dog, but the Babylonians also knew it as a lion as did the ancient Egyptians. The ancient Greeks identified the zodiac lion with the most fearsome one in their mythology, the terrible lion of Nemea.

Hera, queen of the gods, had given this beast a hide so tough that neither iron nor bronze nor stone could pierce it. She brought the lion to Earth to bring about the downfall of her enemy Heracles. It raged across the plain of Nemea, reducing it to a desert. The farmers dared not venture out to guard their animals or work the land. Heracles tracked the lion to its lair, which was a cave with two openings. He blocked one up to stop the lion escaping and, going through the other entrance, he met it face to face. He grasped it by the throat and squeezed with all his strength until the life was choked from its body. Heracles used one of the beast's claws to skin it and then threw the pelt around his shoulders to serve as armour, with the lion's gaping head as a helmet.

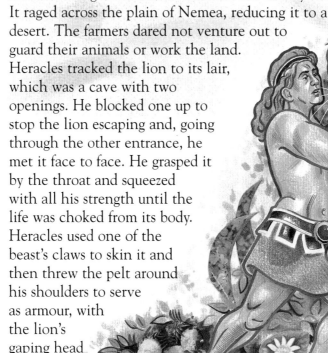

Basic Personality

Leos are renowned for their warm and sunny outlook, and their cheery and generous attitude to other people. Pride and self-importance are common Leo faults and they also have a tendency to laziness.

Ideal Job

Leos are both highly creative and organised and their job should reflect this. They often find work in the theatre and performing arts. Their fondness for being the centre of attention also makes them good lawyers and teachers.

Favourite Hobbies

Ice-skating, dancing and other forms of creative exercise are enjoyable to Leos.

Lifestyle

Leos have a love of luxury and like to be surrounded by the finest of everything. They tend to compete with friends and neighbours to always have the best.

Flower	*Creature*	*Colour*	*Gemstone*	*Food*	*Place*	*People*
Leo flowers include the sunflower, marigold and passion flower.	The lion is the animal most closely associated with Leo, but all big cats share this link.	The colours of the sun and fire are typically Leo: red, gold, orange and amber.	The red ruby is Leo's birthstone.	Leos love food that grows in hot climates: e.g., citrus fruit, pomegranates and olives, as well as hot and spicy food.	Leo countries include Italy, Romania and the Lebanon. Rome is a Leo city.	Leos are well suited to both Sagittareans and Arians.

Virgo

24 August to 23 September

Virgo is an earth sign ruled by Mercury. The outline of its constellation has a human shape, which has been identified with several goddesses: the Babylonian goddess Ishtar; the ancient Greek corn-goddess Demeter; and Demeter's daughter Persephone, whose yearly return from the underworld brought the spring. However, the most common Greek version of Virgo was connected to the maiden goddess Astraea, the bringer of justice.

Wherever Astraea went she filled the souls of those around her with a longing to do good. She made her home on Earth and warmed the hearts of men and women with her kind spirit. This was during the Golden Age, when the world was new. In that happy time the people of the Earth were good and spent their lives free from care. They danced and sang and laughed, for they had no fear of death. The goddess Astraea mingled freely with these gentle mortals, gathering the wisest around her to teach them noble conduct. But time passed and the people of the Golden Age were followed by others of the Age of Silver. Astraea was seen less often among these people, for she did not care to live with men and women who were quarrelsome and uncaring. She fled to the mountains and only descended from time to time in the grey light of evening, to reproach the people for their ignorance and greed. But worse was to come because the Silver Age was followed by an Age of Bronze, in which pitiless people forged weapons of war and murdered each other. Astraea could no longer bear to live among the human race. She flew up to heaven and made her home among the stars and, since that day, cruelty and injustice have flourished in the world.

Basic Personality

Virgoans are organised and practical people, usually highly intelligent and good at expressing themselves. They are often very critical – Virgoans tend to be perfectionists and worry a great deal if a job is not done just so.

Ideal Job

Virgoans have great patience, a fine eye for detail and make excellent craftsmen and designers. They are also good in the caring professions – nursing, teaching or veterinary medicine.

Favourite Hobbies

Health and exercise are very important to a Virgoan and they often get great pleasure from yoga and other alternative therapies.

Lifestyle

Virgoans are almost obsessively tidy and cannot stand being surrounded by other people's mess. They will not get on well with a messy person!

Flower	*Creature*	*Colour*	*Gemstone*	*Food*	*Place*	*People*
All small, brightly coloured flowers are associated with Virgo, like forget-me-nots and buttercups.	All domestic pets, mainly cats and dogs, are connected with Virgo.	Green and dark brown are favourite Virgoan colours.	The Virgoan gemstone is the reddish-brown sardonyx.	Virgoans tend to be very fussy about their food, but are fond of vegetables, especially those grown underground.	Virgoan countries include Greece, the USA and Turkey. Paris and Athens are both Virgoan towns.	A Virgo's best friends tend to be Capricorns or Taureans.

Astrology and medicine

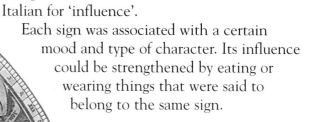

Each zodiac sign is related to a part of the human body. This theory played a major role in medicine until well after medieval times. When the stars were interpreted as being in a position causing bad effects, the corresponding zodiac sign was thought to be weakened. This in turn made the appropriate part of the body unwell. A person born when an unfavourable star was in Aries, for example, would be permanently liable to headaches. Doctors were even reluctant to operate while the moon was in the sign of the affected part of the body, as they believed this would cause further ill effects. Plagues were also believed to be due to the influence of the stars, which is how influenza got its name – the word is Italian for 'influence'.

Each sign was associated with a certain mood and type of character. Its influence could be strengthened by eating or wearing things that were said to belong to the same sign.

Below, a 15th-century illustration of the body's signs. An illness in any part of the body was treated by a herb that belonged to the same sign. Each sign had its own plants, along with colours and gemstones, although various authorities produced differing lists.

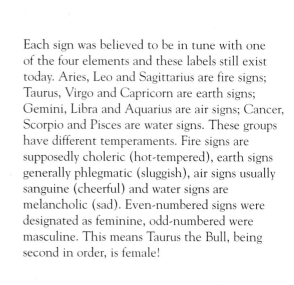

Each sign was believed to be in tune with one of the four elements and these labels still exist today. Aries, Leo and Sagittarius are fire signs; Taurus, Virgo and Capricorn are earth signs; Gemini, Libra and Aquarius are air signs; Cancer, Scorpio and Pisces are water signs. These groups have different temperaments. Fire signs are supposedly choleric (hot-tempered), earth signs generally phlegmatic (sluggish), air signs usually sanguine (cheerful) and water signs are melancholic (sad). Even-numbered signs were designated as feminine, odd-numbered were masculine. This means Taurus the Bull, being second in order, is female!

Left, a 16th-century image of the zodiac signs at work on man. Since the sky seemed to spin round the Earth daily, the position of the signs, seen from any one point, always changed and so, say astrologers, did their influence. New star positions could be described every four minutes.

This image from a 17th-century French engraving (left) is an imaginative portrait of an astronomer. Every part of him refers to his occupation. He holds a pair of compasses and an armillary sphere (an instrument for plotting the position of the sun and planets). The skirts of his coat are bordered with the symbols of the planets and its cuffs are made of the writings of two famous astronomers. His body is covered with the signs of the zodiac, each symbol positioned over the relevant part: Aries the head; Taurus the throat; Gemini the arms; Cancer the chest; Leo the heart; Virgo the stomach; Libra the kidneys; Scorpio the genitals; Sagittarius the thighs; Capricorn the knees; Aquarius the lower legs and Pisces the feet.

Belief in the influence of the signs on humans, animals and crops remained part of country wisdom until quite recently. The farmers' almanac (pictured below) was based on these beliefs and was produced in America in the 18th century.

Libra

24 September to 23 October

Libra is an air sign ruled by Venus. Originally this part of the zodiac was called the Claws of the Scorpion as the constellation of Scorpio is the nearest large group of stars. The name Libra, meaning the scales, does not seem to have been in use before the 2nd century BC and no Greek myth is associated with it. Some people believe that the Egyptians gave the sign this name to honour the ancient Egyptian god Osiris, the king of the dead, who sat in his judgment hall before a huge set of scales. He watched as the heart of each newly dead person was placed in one pan of the scales and balanced against the Feather of Truth in the other. Bad deeds made a heart heavy, so that it weighed down the pan, but a pure heart was lighter than the feather and rose up. Osiris pronounced his judgment according to the verdict of the scales. Good souls went to the happy Field of Reeds; the souls of those with a heavy heart were led away by demons. Other authorities give a more practical reason for thinking the name came from Egypt. At the time of year when the sun reaches the Libran area of the sky, Egyptian officials started their annual weighing of the harvest for tax purposes. However, still others state that there is no reason to think the scales are an Egyptian concept. They could just as well symbolise the equal length of day and night at this time of the year.

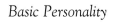

Basic Personality

Librans love harmony; they are the peace-makers of the zodiac. They are also charming, romantic and witty. Indecision is the main Libran fault – they tend to change their mind about everything from day to day.

Ideal Job

Librans' skill at resolving conflict makes them suited to careers such as diplomacy, law and politics, although they also have a creative streak making them talented at art, poetry and music.

Favourite Hobbies

Many Librans enjoy painting and music in their free time. Their ability to see both sides of a story makes them keen debaters.

Lifestyle

Librans have strong opinions on how their surroundings should look – they like to decorate rooms to their own individual taste.

Flower	Creature	Colour	Gemstone	Food	Places	People
Roses are traditionally associated with Libra, and so are all blue flowers, such as bluebells and violets.	Snakes, lizards and other small reptiles are Libran.	The Libran colour is blue, in all its many shades.	Sapphire and jade are Libran precious stones.	Librans are partial to all types of fruit, but berries in particular. They often have a sweet tooth and love confectionery.	Canada, Japan and Tibet are amongst the Libran countries.	Librans get on really well with Aquarians and Geminis.

Scorpio

24 October to 22 November

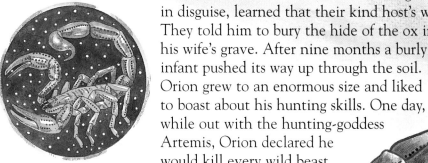

Scorpio is a water sign, ruled by Mars and associated with war and death. The constellation of Scorpio looks a little like a scorpion with its tail raised ready to strike. It was known by that name by the Babylonians and the ancient Greeks. The zodiac scorpion is connected with the hunter Orion, after whom a brilliant group of stars is named.

Orion came into the world in an unusual way. Two travellers knocked one day at the door of a poor farmer and asked for shelter. He welcomed them in and killed an ox for their dinner. The strangers, who were the gods Zeus and Hermes in disguise, learned that their kind host's wife was dead and he was childless. They told him to bury the hide of the ox in his wife's grave. After nine months a burly infant pushed its way up through the soil. Orion grew to an enormous size and liked to boast about his hunting skills. One day, while out with the hunting-goddess Artemis, Orion declared he would kill every wild beast upon the Earth. His words were overheard by Mother Earth, who was furious at this threat to her creatures. She called up a monstrous scorpion to chase Orion. He attacked with arrows and a sword, but no weapon could pierce its shell. To escape, Orion dived into the sea, but the scorpion followed and stung him fatally in the foot. The grieving Artemis placed Orion among the stars and the monster scorpion still chases him in the sky, never quite reaching him.

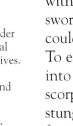

Basic Personality

Scorpios are full of energy, honest, determined and adventurous. They are also very emotional and sensitive people. Jealousy is a major Scorpio downfall, along with secrecy and obsessiveness.

Ideal Job

Scorpios work well under pressure and are natural researchers and detectives. They do well in engineering, mining and the armed services.

Favourite Hobbies

The martial arts are suited to Scorpios, along with most energetic team sports.

Lifestyle

The natural secrecy of Scorpios makes them very protective of their privacy. They tend to put locks on their doors, along with plenty of 'Keep Out' signs.

Flower	Creature	Colour	Gemstone	Food	Places	People
Rhododendrons, geraniums and honeysuckle are Scorpio flowers.	Most insects are associated with Scorpio.	Scorpio colours include dark red and maroon.	The opal is the traditional Scorpio gemstone.	Scorpios enjoy most strong flavoured food but love garlic and onions in particular.	Scorpio countries include Morocco and Norway.	Scorpios are very well suited to Pisceans and to Cancerians.

*I*ndia, Persia and the Islamic world

*T*he zodiacs of India and the Middle East are closely related to the western one. In ancient times the Indians had a zodiac with twenty-seven divisions which measured the progress of the moon. The western zodiac, linked to the 'movement' of the sun, reached India via translations of Greek astrology in the 2nd-3rd centuries AD. The Indians, who already interpreted changes in the stars as omens, adopted and adapted western astrology to suit their needs. They subdivided the signs further and added two extra 'stars' called the nodes of the moon. The influences of the stars were also reassessed to make them more meaningful to the Indian way of life. In India a great deal of attention centres around the branch of astrology concerning the most favourable moment for beginning something, e.g., a war, a marriage, a journey, etc. The moment when the decision is made to do a deed is recorded, and the horoscope for that instant is then studied.

Macara

Kumbha

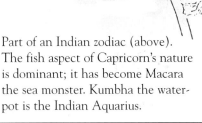

Part of an Indian zodiac (above). The fish aspect of Capricorn's nature is dominant; it has become Macara the sea monster. Kumbha the water-pot is the Indian Aquarius.

A 17th-century Persian portrait of Sagittarius (below) taken from a textbook of astrology. It shows the position of the stars in the constellation Sagittarius, after which the sign was named. The outlines of the archer, with flying turban-ends, have been drawn to coincide with them.

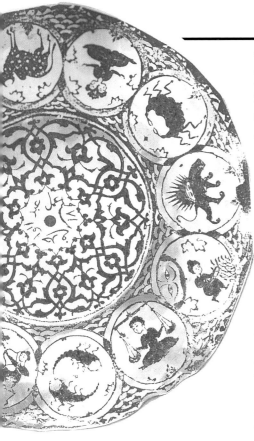

When the Arabs captured Alexandria, in Egypt, in the 7th century they became fascinated by the astrological tradition they discovered there. They quickly absorbed and developed its theories, becoming skilled astronomers and astronomical instrument makers. A large collection of astrological writings was stored in the great library of Baghdad in the 9th century. Arab Spain also became a centre for astrological studies, specialising in the use of astrology in medicine. The Islamic faith forbids the representation of the human form, so in place of the Twins of Gemini the Islamic zodiac often shows two peacocks, Virgo becomes a sheaf of corn and the image for Aquarius is a mule with two baskets.

Meanwhile, in the Dark Ages, Europe was cut off from contact with Greek culture and scholarly astrology declined.

A 10th-century Arabic astrolabe (above), an instrument for measuring the position of the stars. Its use was known to the Greeks in the 2nd century AD but it was the Arabs who perfected it.

A 16th-century Persian plate decorated with the signs of the zodiac (above). They are all recognisable, with some realistic touches: Aquarius is drawing water from a well; Capricorn has shed its fish's tail and perches on a peak as goats do and the sun is glowing behind its ruling sign, Leo.

The two sides of a 16th-century gold coin issued by the Indian emperor Jahangir (above). It shows the twins image of Gemini.

A page from a 13th-century Arabic manuscript which discusses the effects of the meeting of stars in the same sign (right). The main illustration shows the Moon, represented by a full-faced woman, and Jupiter, a nobleman, meeting in the the sign of Sagittarius.

Sagittarius

23 November to 21 December

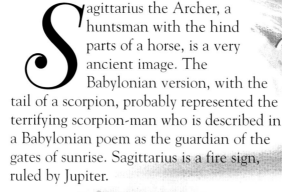

Sagittarius the Archer, a huntsman with the hind parts of a horse, is a very ancient image. The Babylonian version, with the tail of a scorpion, probably represented the terrifying scorpion-man who is described in a Babylonian poem as the guardian of the gates of sunrise. Sagittarius is a fire sign, ruled by Jupiter.

The ancient Greeks saw Sagittarius as a centaur. Centaurs were unruly creatures, half man and half horse, who lived wild in the mountains. They were far from friendly and would come galloping down the mountain slopes brandishing uprooted trees as weapons. Many stories were told of their bad behaviour, which became much worse if they were given wine. However, there was one centaur quite unlike the rest. This was the noble and immortal centaur Chiron, the one most often identified as the centaur of the zodiac. The hero Heracles was his friend, but it was through this friendship that Chiron met his end. Heracles, resting in Chiron's cave one day, set down his bow and quiver. Chiron admired them and accidentally got an arrow lodged in his hoof. The arrow tips had been dipped in poisonous blood so the wound was incurable. As Chiron could not die he suffered unendingly, until the god Zeus took pity on him and allowed him to lose his immortality.

Basic Personality

Sagittarians are bold, lively and always live for the moment. They are curious and enthusiastic about life, making them good scholars. Unfortunately, Sagittarians are fond of taking risks and can get themselves into trouble this way. They tend not to think things through very well.

Ideal Job

An office job is not for a Sagittarian! Anything which allows them to travel or provides a varied environment is suitable, e.g., air hostess, explorer or travel agent.

Favourite Hobbies

Horse-riding, mountaineering, hangliding and anything else challenging and adventurous.

Lifestyle

Sagittarians are usually messy and disorganised. They are often far too busy with their exciting hobbies and pursuits to care about housework.

Flower	Creature	Colour	Gemstone	Food	Place	People
Dandelions and carnations are true Sagittarian flowers.	Animals that have traditionally been hunted, such as deer, are ruled by Sagittarius.	Rich, dark purple is commonly associated with Sagittarius.	The Sagittarian gemstone is the topaz.	Sagittarians love cooking and food. Favourites include grapefruit, raisins and celery.	Australia is thought to be a Sagittarian country.	Arians and Leos make the best friends for Sagittarians.

Capricorn

22 December to 20 January

Capricorn is an earth sign. It is commonly shown as a goat with the tail of a fish. One of the titles of the Babylonian god Ea was the 'antelope of the ocean', half animal and half fish, which seems to be the origin of this creature. The ancient Egyptians also saw this constellation as a goat.

Capricorn was often identified with the Greek god Pan, the protector of shepherds and their flocks. He was a half-man, half-goat creature, with small horns on his head and the hind legs of a goat. Pan was normally a friendly god, but he could be wild and unpredictable. It was dangerous to meet him in the heat of midday, as he was liable to fierce rages which filled people with an irrational terror which gets its name from him – 'panic'.

Alternatively, Capricorn is sometimes said to be Aigokeros, the son of Pan. Aigokeros was half god, half goat. When the gods fought a terrible battle with their enemies the Titans, he made a trumpet from a conch shell and blew such a blast that the Titans fled. To mark their victory, the gods gave him a fish's tail.

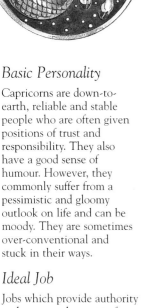

Basic Personality

Capricorns are down-to-earth, reliable and stable people who are often given positions of trust and responsibility. They also have a good sense of humour. However, they commonly suffer from a pessimistic and gloomy outlook on life and can be moody. They are sometimes over-conventional and stuck in their ways.

Ideal Job

Jobs which provide authority and command respect often suit a Capricorn, including being a policeman or woman, lawyer or business person.

Favourite Hobbies

Anything which demands perseverance and stamina, for example, long-distance running and mountain climbing. Capricorns are usually keen on literature and music.

Lifestyle

A Capricorn's home is not usually glamorous, but is always comfortable, practical and relaxing.

Flower	*Creature*	*Colour*	*Gemstone*	*Food*	*Places*	*People*
Ivy and pansies are Capricorn plants.	The Capricorn animal is the goat and all other cloven-hoofed animals.	Capricorn colours are usually dark, including dark grey, dark green and brown.	Amethyst and turquoise are the gemstones commonly associated with Capricorn.	Capricorns like plain, wholesome foods like potatoes, pasta and rice.	India and Mexico are Capricorn countries as are their capital cities, Delhi and Mexico City.	Taureans and Virgoans usually get on very well with Capricorns.

The Chinese zodiac

The Chinese zodiac has almost no connection with the western signs. Instead of representing parts of the sky, each of the twelve gives its name to a year and to an 'hour' (two normal hours). The names are in a fixed order: the year of the Rat, Ox, Tiger, Hare, Dragon, Snake, Horse, Sheep, Monkey, Cock, Dog and the Pig. The year 2000 is the year of the Dragon, 2001 the year of the Snake and so on. The hours of the day follow in the same way. The Rat rules the midnight 'hour' which runs from 11pm to 1am. Chinese astrologers believe that each person forms a small part of the great pattern of the universe. From the animal of a person's year of birth they interpret their character and offer advice on how to live in harmony with the pattern that year establishes.

This bronze mirror-back (right) of the T'ang dynasty (AD 618-906) has four creatures at its centre, representing the four quarters of the sky: the Green Dragon of the East, the Red Bird of South, the White Tiger of the West and the Black Turtle of the North. Around them run the twelve animals of the Chinese zodiac.

Rat people are good company, quick-witted, good talkers and good problem solvers.

Ox people are slow and steady, honest and reliable. They do not give up in the face of difficulty.

Tiger people are natural leaders, brave and sure of themselves.

Hare people are sensitive, kind hearted and like to help others. They are often healers or carers.

Dragon people are live wires, restless, full of ideas and quick to seize an opportunity.

Snake people are clever and full of good sense but quiet and reserved.

Horse people are strong, trustworthy and energetic. They love outdoor activities and make loyal friends.

Sheep people are thoughtful, often gifted and very patient.

Monkey people are impatient, but are resourceful and never in trouble long.

Cock people are extravagant and like a good time.

Dog people make good hosts. They are warm, humorous and good at making others feel relaxed.

Pig people are easy-going and like a comfortable life.

There are several Chinese folk tales about the choosing of the animals for the zodiac. One story tells that the Emperor of the Heavens decided that the years needed names. He summoned the animals to him and announced that those who paid him homage would each have a year named after them. Twelve stepped forward, one by one, and that is how the number, names and order of the years were fixed. Another story tells how the animals held a race to decide their order in the list. The last part of the race was across a river. At this point the rat pleaded that it was afraid of the water so the good-natured ox gave it a lift on its back. On the other bank the rat leapt down and raced ahead to claim first place.

In another version of the tale the rat said to the ox that first place should go to whichever of them people said was bigger. Of course the ox agreed. They went to town, but people took no notice of the ox. They were used to seeing oxen, but to see a rat walking beside one was very strange. 'Look at that huge rat!' they cried. The poor ox had to agree that the rat had won.

Aquarius

21 January to 19 February

Aquarius is an air sign, ruled by Saturn. Aquarius the Water-Pourer originates from the life-giving, water-pouring gods of Babylon and Egypt. The ancient Greeks believed that Aquarius was Ganymede, the young cup-bearer to the gods on Mount Olympus. Ganymede was the son of Laomedon, king of Troy. He was such a beautiful child that he caught the eye of Zeus, king of the gods. Zeus sent an eagle to snatch the child and carry him off to Olympus, where he became a favourite with the gods and was made immortal. Naturally, Ganymede's parents were upset at the theft of their son. To put matters right Zeus gave Laomedon a magnificent present, a pair of amazingly swift horses that were the offspring of the North Wind and were immortal. This was not enough for the king and his greed caused his downfall. Laomedon wanted to build his city a defensive wall, so he hired the sea god, Poseidon, to help. But when the work was finished the king would not pay him. The furious god sent a sea monster to eat Laomedon's people and to spit sea-water over his fields. The Greek hero Heracles offered to kill the monster in return for the immortal horses. Laomedon agreed, so Heracles leapt down the monster's throat and killed it from inside. The king went back on his word and would not let him have the horses so Heracles collected an army, invaded the city and killed Laomedon and all of his sons that he could find. Watching from Olympus, the gods rejoiced that Ganymede was safe with them.

Basic Personality

Aquarians are friendly and concerned about those less fortunate than themselves. They are also optimistic and independent. However, Aquarians are often accused of being unemotional and detached and they can be very unpredictable.

Ideal Job

Aquarians make good communicators and suit jobs in areas such as television or radio. They often make excellent charity workers and counsellors.

Favourite Hobbies

Aquarians often enjoy conversation and debating and are also drawn to creative and inventive pursuits such as art and sculpture.

Lifestyle

Aquarians like to experiment with their surroundings so their homes and rooms are often full of strange and quirky objects and decor.

Flower	*Creature*	*Colour*	*Gemstone*	*Food*	*Places*	*People*
The orchid is an Aquarian plant, as are most fruit trees.	Aquarius is the ruler of birds which are capable of long distance flight, such as the albatross.	Electric blue and turquoise are the key Aquarius colours.	Aquamarine is the Aquarian gemstone.	Aquarians love all types of exciting and foreign food and are always prepared to try something new.	Russia, Sweden and Poland are all Aquarian countries.	Aquarians generally make good friends of Geminis and Librans.

Pisces

20 February to 20 March

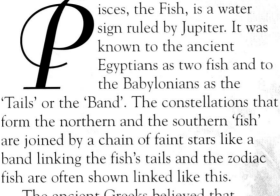

Pisces, the Fish, is a water sign ruled by Jupiter. It was known to the ancient Egyptians as two fish and to the Babylonians as the 'Tails' or the 'Band'. The constellations that form the northern and the southern 'fish' are joined by a chain of faint stars like a band linking the fish's tails and the zodiac fish are often shown linked like this.

The ancient Greeks believed that the fish of the zodiac were the two that helped in the birth of a goddess. Two fish swimming in the River Euphrates came across a huge floating egg. They bobbed it along with their heads towards the bank and pushed it onto land. A dove then flew down from the sky and spread her wings over the egg to hatch it. After some days the Syrian goddess Atargatis stepped from the shell. Atargatis was the goddess of fruitfulness who made the crops grow. She was portrayed as half woman and half fish because she was born from water. She asked the king of the gods to honour the fish by placing them in the sky. These fish actually belong to Middle Eastern myth but the ancient Greeks liked to think that foreign gods were versions of their own. They regarded Atargatis as their goddess of love, Aphrodite, under another name.

A variation on this story connects the zodiac fish with the disguises the gods took when they fled the monster Typhon. Aphrodite and her son Eros turned themselves into fish and hid in the Nile. In order not be separated they tied their tails together.

Basic Personality

Pisceans are very creative and imaginative. They are also understanding people who are extremely kind and compassionate. Disorganisation and an inability to face up to reality are typical Piscean failings. They also tend to be secretive and weak-willed.

Ideal Job

Pisceans should work in creative areas if possible, or in the caring professions. They tend to make superb actors.

Favourite Hobbies

If a Piscean does not work in highly creative areas, he will often get immense pleasure from writing poetry or playing music.

Lifestyle

Because Pisceans are such caring people, their homes tend to be full of friends and relatives who need help of one sort or another.

Flower	Creature	Colour	Gemstone	Food	Places	People
The water lily and the willow are naturally Piscean.	Fish are Piscean creatures as are any other animals which live in water.	Soft sea green is the typical Piscean colour.	The gem associated with Pisces is the magical opal.	Pisceans often enjoy watery foods such as melon, cucumber and lettuce.	Portugal and Scandinavia are Piscean places.	A Piscean's best friends are often Cancerians or Scorpios.

The modern zodiac

Is there any truth in astrology? Astrology grew from the ancient belief that since the Earth was at the centre of the universe, the circling of the stars around it must have meaning. In the 16th century, the astronomer Copernicus showed that the Earth was just one of several planets that circled the sun. This destroyed the original reason for believing that the movements of the 'stars' affect events on Earth. Other than the sun's light and warmth and the moon's gravitational pull on the tides, modern scientists can discover no physical means by which the constellations and planets influence the world.

Astrologers argue that they study the relative positions of the 'stars' as seen from the Earth and that these are the same whether it is the Earth or the sun that is at the centre of things. This is true. However, many people see no reason why these relationships should have the intricate web of meaning that astrologers detect in them, or any meaning at all. Astrologers state they are proved right because their interpretations are right. If they are incorrect, then it is purely a matter of misinterpretation.

Above, a portrait of the Polish astronomer Copernicus. His theory of the solar system was published in 1543.

Above, a telescope used by the 17th-century Italian, Galileo, who confirmed Copernicus' theory.

From the 17th century onwards scientific people increasingly doubted the truth of astrology. The signs of the zodiac were used as decorative designs. The Leo above adorns 18th-century Russian panelling.

A late 17th-century satirical print shows a man being fooled by astrologers (left). It is implied that they are no better than bogus magicians. A jester is mocking the man behind his back.

Astrologers no longer claim that the 'stars' foretell anything, as that would deny the concept of free will. Instead, it is said that the signs of the zodiac shape our character and exert favourable or unfavourable influences upon our daily life. How do the influences of the stars reach us? Astrologers argue that it is not necessary to search out the effects – the stars do not cause anything, they only indicate. Humans respond to them because all things are affected by 'the rhythm of the universe'. There is very little scientific basis to astrology. However, if you believe in magic, you may believe in the influence of the signs of the zodiac.

A zodiac ceiling decoration dated 1898 (above) to compare with the ancient Egyptian one on page 13. The more recent one has the sun at its centre. It decorates the ceiling of a music room in the Villa Stuck, at Munich in Germany.

A sky 'map', showing the constellatons in picture form, makes an effective decoration for a round table top. This detail from an Italian table is from the 1950s (right).

Astrology 'facts'

Horoscope for a city

In the ancient world, Babylonian astrologers were known as Chaldeans (from the Babylonian province of Chaldea) and this term soon came to be applied to any astrologer of Middle Eastern origins. 'Chaldeans' travelled widely, taking the beliefs and skills of astrology to many lands. It was in their interests to boost its reputation as a source of knowledge on every subject under the sun – kings and princes were eager to pay for the services of such well-informed advisers. The Chaldeans claimed that humans were not alone in having a 'moment of birth' for which a horoscope could be made, cities had them too. In 312 BC, Seleucus I, a Macedonian ruler imposed on the Babylonians, planned to create a new city. He took the precaution of asking his Chaldeans to work out the most favourable moment for its 'birth', the moment of laying the first stone. The Chaldeans met together and decided that the new city was a bad idea. It would eclipse the glory of Babylon and lead to its ruin. So they selected the worst possible moment and advised the king to found his city then. Seleucus gave orders accordingly, but it is said that the builders, wanting to please him with their eagerness, started the work before the stated time. This provided the city, quite accidentally, with an extremely lucky 'moment of birth'. It was easy to believe, with hindsight, that the moment had been lucky for the city flourished and Babylon decayed. The astrologers certainly thought this was the builders' fault.

Awkward questions

In the past, astrologers' claims to be able to predict the future exposed them to certain dangers. Powerful rulers were sometimes unable to resist the temptation to prove them wrong. They would ask an astrologer to predict the date of his own death and then execute him immediately to prove that he had been wrong. Alexander the Great showed that he was born to be one of the greatest conquerors in history by thinking up this little game when he was only twelve. According to legend, his tutor was an Egyptian called Nectanebo who was favoured by Alexander's mother. Alexander is said to have tipped Nectanebo over a cliff to prove that the astrologer could not foretell his own death.

Astrological answers

Any astrologer serving an unpredictable ruler needed to have an answer for the trick question: "Can you predict your own death?" It would never do to say no as that would lead to dismissal for incompetence. The cunning astrologer to whom the emperor Tiberius put this question replied that the emperor would outlive him by a day. Another astrologer, in a similar situation, replied, "I stand now in the greatest danger of death." To execute him would prove him right.

An astrologer who was right

According to ancient astrologers, attempts to prove them wrong were liable to backfire. The astrologer Asclation was asked by the emperor Domitian if he could foretell his own death. "I am doomed to be torn to pieces by dogs," the astrologer replied. The emperor ordered that he should die at once by crucifixion. But while the astrologer was being nailed to the cross a thunderstorm of terrifying force arose. His executioners ran for shelter, as did the keepers of some ferocious circus dogs. The dogs killed the astrologer – presumably to his satisfaction since they had proved him right!

The emperor Domitian was extremely superstitious and took all predictions literally. Because an astrologer had told him he would die by iron he refused to have a guard of honour which carried spears. He checked the date and hour of birth of anyone remotely likely to be his rival and on such evidence put many innocent people to death. It is said that the time of his own death was predicted by astrologers – the fifth hour of the eighteenth day of September, AD 96. When the day came, Domitian was in a state of panic. He sent a servant again and again to get the exact time. The servant finally grew tired of this and told his master that the hour was over. Hugely relieved, the emperor went to take a bath. While he was relaxing, an attendant who had offered to read to him there drew out a hidden dagger and stabbed him to death.

Choosing an astrologer

Frederick II, who was Holy Roman Emperor in the 13th century, employed a succession of court astrologers. It is said that he liked to test them before appointing them. On one occasion he said to a new applicant, "By which gate shall I choose to leave the castle today?" The astrologer gave his reply in writing, sealed it and asked the emperor to read it after leaving the castle. The emperor ordered

a hole to be made in the castle wall and went out through it, without using any gate. Then he opened the sealed reply which read, 'The emperor will leave today by a new way.' Presumably the astrologer got the job.

A false alarm

In AD 1186 people throughout Europe were in a state of panic. Astrologers had discovered that in September of that year all the planets would come together in the sign of Libra, a rare coincidence which signalled a dreadful disaster. Since Libra was an air sign, terrible storms were predicted. People dug underground burrows to hide in until the worst was over and church services were held to beg God to redirect the stars. When September came it proved to be mild throughout. The astrologers claimed they were still more right than wrong. Some evil effect could be expected, they had merely misjudged its nature. When, in the following year, Crusaders in the Holy Land were badly defeated, astrologers declared that this was the evil effect they had been expecting.

Some astrological tips

Medieval medical advice was commonly influenced by the star signs. If you take a laxative when the moon is in Capricorn it will give you constipation. When Mars is in Taurus it will produce sore throats. If Mars is in Libra while Saturn is in Capricorn the kidneys and the hips may be in trouble. Nettles, a plant of Aries, should be used for treating headaches and elderflower, a Taurean plant, treats sunburn. Diseases of the liver, ruled by Jupiter, will be neutralised by plants under the influence of Mercury.

Glossary

Almanac A book issued annually, containing astronomical information about the coming year. It includes a calendar showing the phases of the moon, a weather forecast and astrological predictions.

Astrolabe An instrument which was used to measure the altitude of heavenly bodies.

Celestial Belonging to the sky.

Conch A large sea snail.

Constellation A recognisable group of stars.

Degree One 360th of the circumference of a circle.

Euphrates A river flowing through Syria and Iraq. Mespotamian civilisation flourished between the Euphrates and Tigris rivers from before 3000 BC.

Falconer Someone who trains hawks for hunting.

Finial An ornament positioned on the peak or corners of a roof.

Grafting Inserting a shoot from one plant into the stem of another with stronger roots. The host plant is cut back so that its roots feed the the grafted shoot.

Heavenly bodies Any non-man-made objects in the sky.

Hemisphere A half of the Earth. The equator divided the world into southern and northern hemispheres.

Hermes The messenger of the gods in ancient Greek mythology. The Romans called him Mercury.

Horoscope A chart of the sun's, moon's and planets' positions in the zodiac at a particular time, as seen from a particular point on the globe.

Middle East The countries around and beyond the south-eastern end of the Mediterranean.

Omen Any circumstance or happening which is thought to foretell good or bad fortune.

Oracle A sacred place where a god was believed to answer questions, usually through the mouth of a priest or priestess who spoke in a trance.

Pelt The skin and hair or fur of an animal.

Penance A task undertaken to show remorse for a sin.

Planet A heavenly body that revolves around a star. The planets in the solar system revolve around the sun. Earth is a primary planet because it revolves directly round the sun. The moon is a secondary planet (a satellite) because it revolves around a primary one.

Sacrifice A ritual in which an offering is made to honour or appease a god.

Sanskrit An ancient Indian language, still in written use today.

Scorpion A poisonous creature, commonly thought of as an insect but actually belonging to the spider family.

Star A heavenly body that gives out light, as opposed to a planet which only reflects the light from a star. The sun is a star.

Index